First edition: First printing

ISBN 978-1517337735

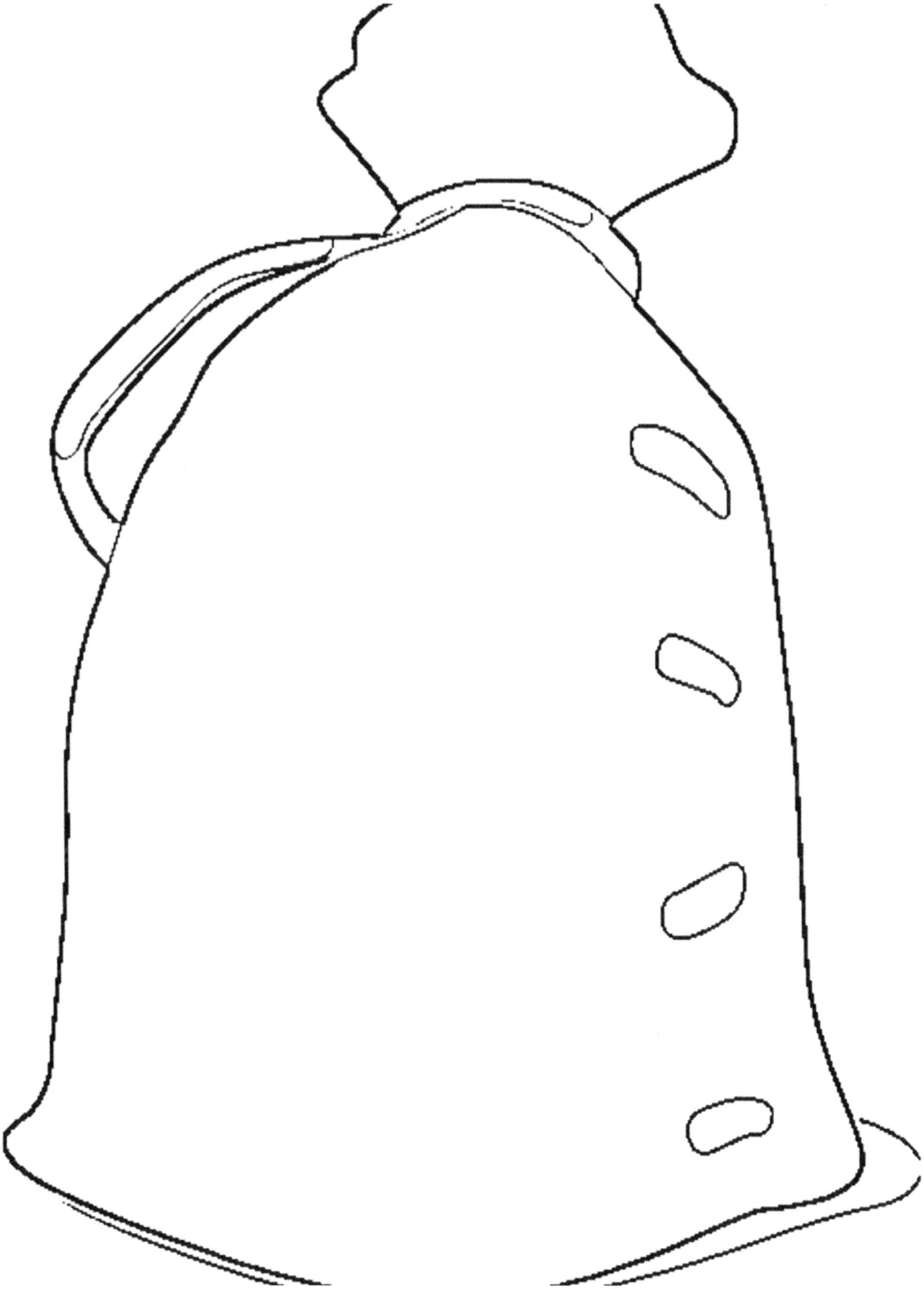

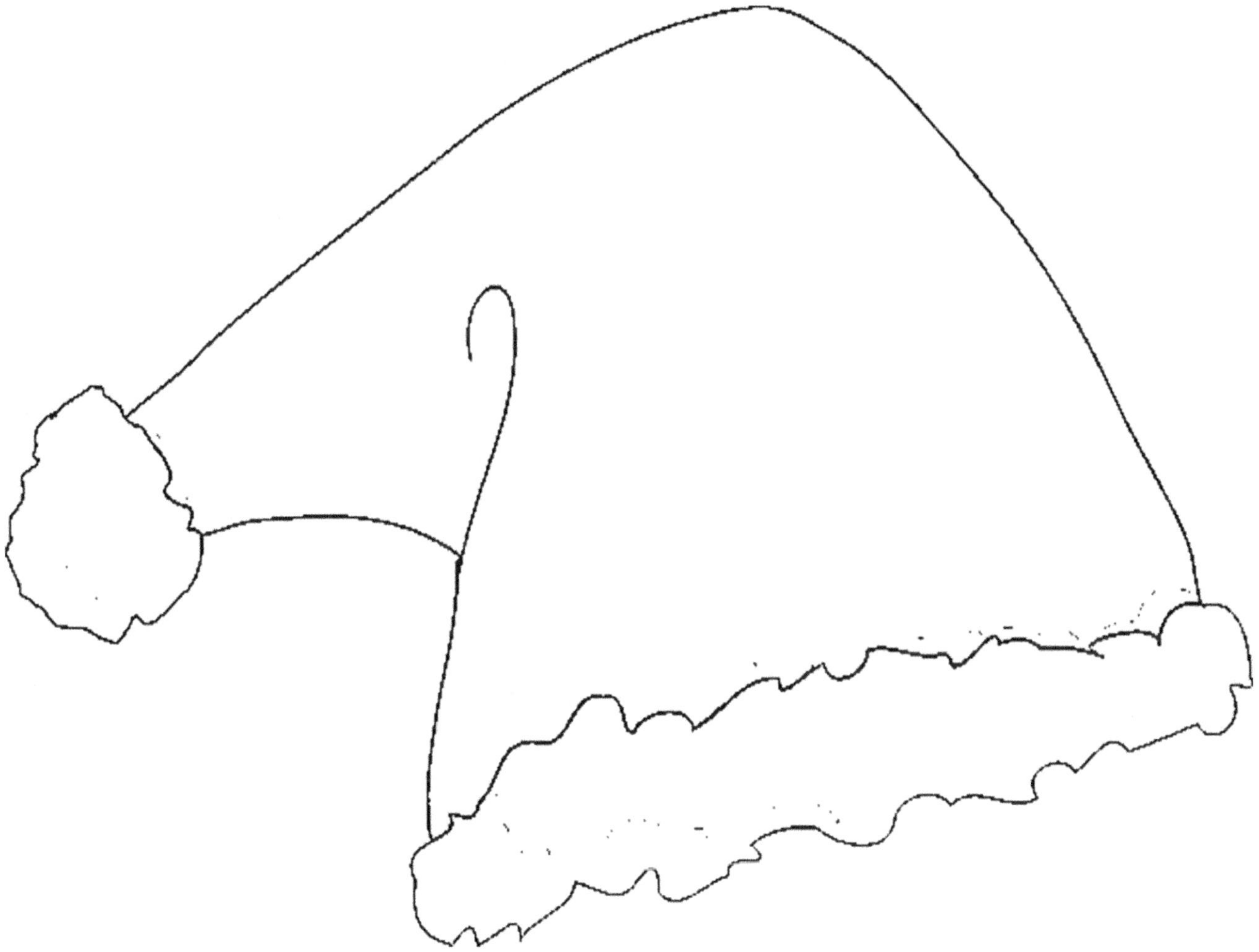

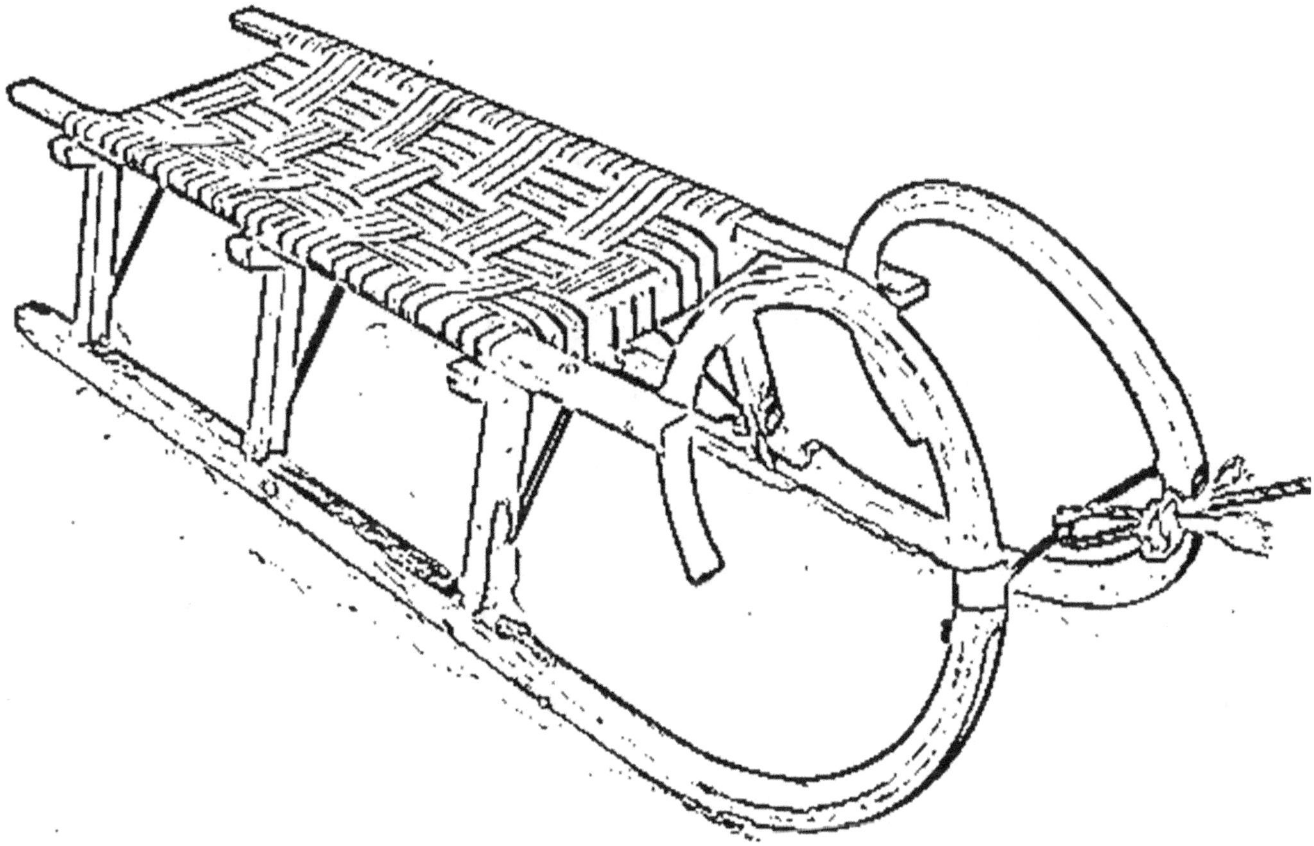

MN

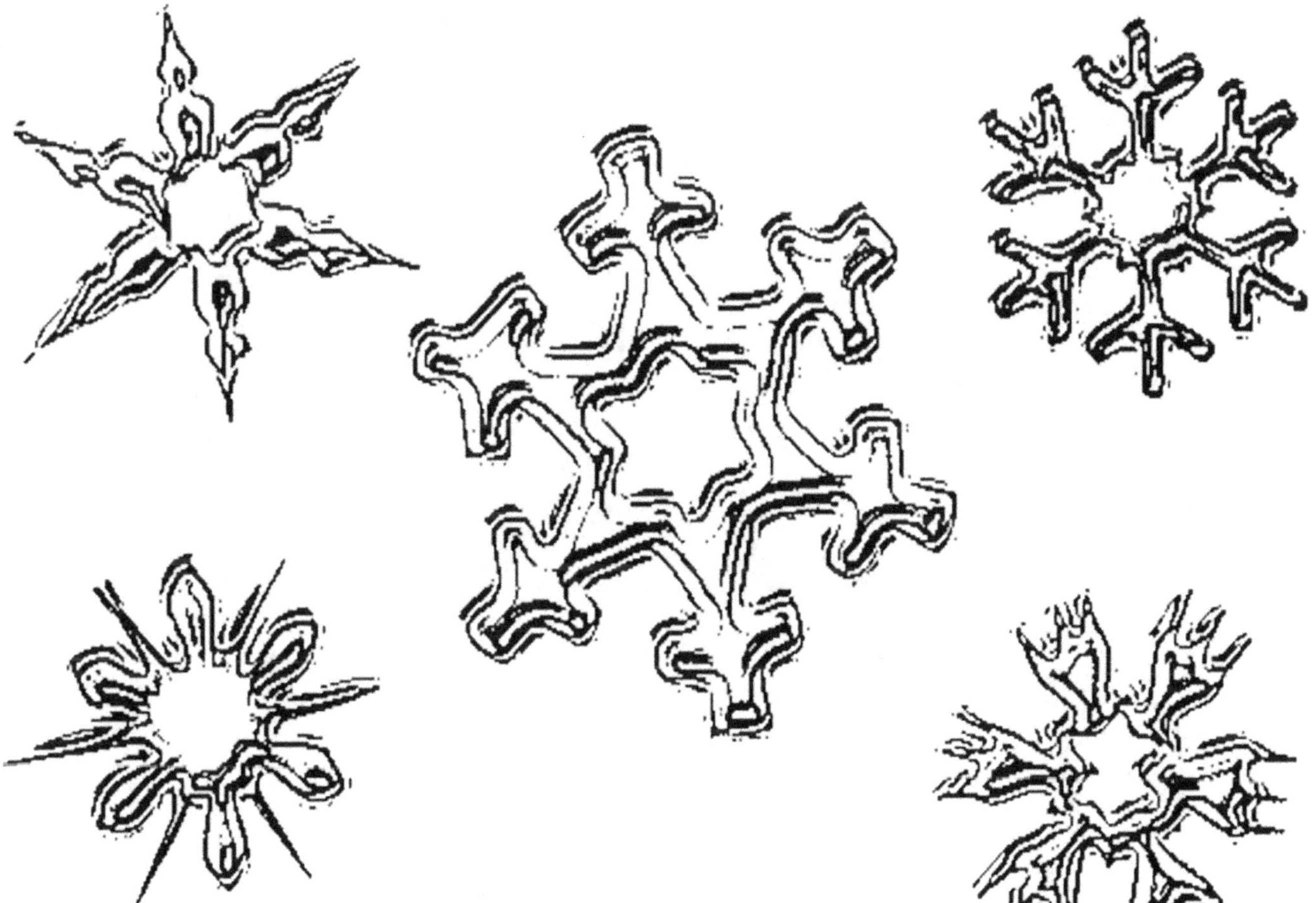

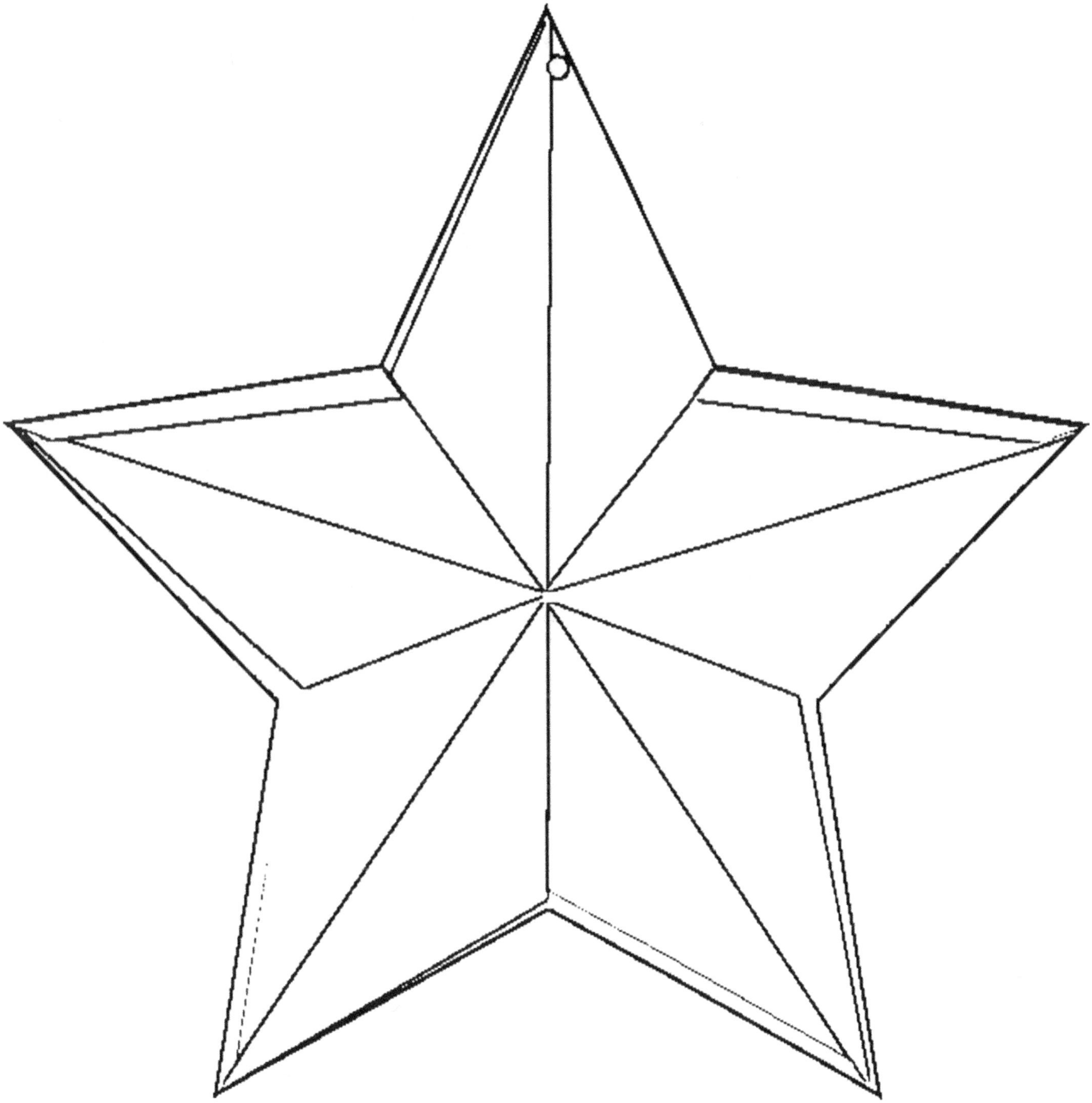

www.ingramcontent.com/pod-product-compliance
Lightning Source LLC
Chambersburg PA
CBHW081154280526
45787CB00008B/3324
9781517337735